Table of Contents

Chapter 1: Anxiety's Roots / The Starting Point

My Story

I had my first panic attack at the age of eleven. Like an alarming number of modern youth, I was rushed to the hospital with chest pain, shortness of breath, and a skyrocketing heart rate.

The diagnosis: anxiety. Although I had not been conscious of any worry at the time of my attack, the doctors could find nothing physically wrong with me.

"This," the doctors said, "is quite common." Later when working in a pediatric emergency department, I would see it all the time: teens presenting with debilitating *physical* symptoms because of anxiety. People coming of age in our increasingly high-pressure culture are developing paralyzing problems for purely psychological reasons more and more often.

Indeed, studies have found that today, anxiety and depression disorders are five to eight times more common than they were 50 years ago. And we as a society only seem to be getting more anxious.[1]

Why should this be so?

Research has turned up many factors possibly contributing to our modern anxiety levels. Contributing factors likely include an increase in competing social demands, lack of physical activity, changes to our diets, and the constant presence of technology which interacts in some worrisome ways with the motivation and anxiety systems in our brains.[2]

Most of the suspected causes, I think, can be summarized like this: we were made for a very different environment than the one we now live in.

Our stress and anxiety responses evolved to deal with our ancestors' biggest problems: things like famine, and getting chased by lions. We were made to react strongly to potential threats, because potential threats could be deadly. We were not made for a world where "threats" such as emails from our boss and Internet arguments were coming at us hundred times a day.

Equally problematic, the automatic responses our bodies have to help us to escape lions or starvation don't work so well for dealing with modern sources of stress such as, deadlines, exams, and social anxiety. If anything, our body's reactions encouraging "fight or flight" and calorie hoarding can make it harder for us to manage our lives in productive ways.

This means that we must be mindful in how we respond to stress – and in how we sculpt our own thoughts and feelings. There are many tools available to us to build better lives for ourselves, but our society has widely failed to acknowledge these.

I myself have often struggled to admit that I might need to *do* more to combat my anxiety, rather than just thinking it away. Often when a panic attack or a sudden feeling of burnout hits, my instant response is frustration. Why must this be happening to me? Why can't I just *make it go away?*

It turns out that we can't simply "will" our anxiety away for a few reasons. The brain and body are physical organs - they have physical mechanisms.

To work with our brains, we have to take the same approach we would for working with any machine: we have to know when to press the right buttons, what gears to grease, and how to re-align an axle. And the actions we can take to manage our moods and thought processes are often physical - actions that affect our body chemistry, rather than just "thinking good thoughts."

Of course, brains are *more* than machines - but just because they produce such wonderfully complex and vivid things as emotions, doesn't mean they belong to some other realm of pure thought, as Western thought has typically assumed.

The idea that you can just "think yourself to wellness" because the mind is purely mental, not physical, is the root of many evils in the Western world. For centuries, it has encouraged European and American thinkers to ignore ways we could change our systems of living to make them better, in favor of simply suggesting that those who have trouble with the current system are somehow weak or morally deficient.

In fact, people who experience anxiety and depression are not

In the modern world, we're often unaware of when these messages are sent - who would have thought, for example, that checking your emails can cause your body to send similar chemical messages to being chased by a lion?

This realization tells us that anxiety is very real. It's not just a figment of your imagination - it is biochemically the same as being chased by a lion. But it *also* makes it more manageable; simply trying *not* to be anxious hasn't been working because anxiety is not a mental thing. It's a physical thing, and by being aware of the physical ways we can change our mood, we can change anxiety with much more success than simply trying to think positive.

Some things can be both a cause of and a response to stress. For example, we develop tense muscles as a result of stress; our brains then perceive that our muscles are tense and go "oh no, we've tensed our muscles, we must be facing a threat!" For this reason, our anxiety doesn't just shape our body's behavior; the state of our body also shapes our level of anxiety!

Here are some important messengers that our brain and body release in response to stress:

Cortisol

I like to think of as the "famine hormone," (although it's not that simple - cortisol has many fight-or-flight effects as well, but it is more associated with chronic rather than acute stress).

Among other things, it causes us to crave high-calorie foods, and directly raises our blood sugar by changing the metabolism of the liver. It also suppresses immune function, because fighting infection isn't the first priority when you are starving.

Reducing levels of cortisol by giving your body "all clear, we're safe" signals such as sleeping enough and exercising to burn off adrenaline is *incredibly* helpful to well-being.

Studies (and my own personal experience) have shown that we are naturally inclined to make healthier diet choices and decisions that are better for our long-term goals when our cortisol levels are low.

This is because high cortisol levels make our bodies "think" that our linked with our identities - to the point that I myself avoided therapy and psychiatric medication for years, because my feelings were my own and I didn't want them changed.

It took realizing that I was being *controlled* by my feelings - that they were holding me back from doing things I *wanted* to do, and that these conscious desires were at least as crucial to who I was as involuntary feelings - for me to realize that perhaps I would be *more* myself if I accepted more tools in my quest to take the *actions* that I *wanted* to take.

I'd been raised in a very Western philosophy that taught that the body was little more than a nuisance to the mind - a temporary vessel the mind was trapped in, which was mostly just a source of limitation and evil temptation.

"The world, the flesh, and the devil" was a popular saying in my church, harkening back to the days of Plato, who strongly influenced Western thought and who taught that the mind belonged to a higher realm than the body and was inherently separate from it.

But the scientists who taught my classes said that the body *created* the mind - that all of our thoughts and feelings arose from *physical* processes which had *evolved* to deal with our natural world. I had to study more about this - if what the scientists were saying was true, it could be very powerful knowledge!

Anyone who's tried psychiatric medication and had a bad experience can tell you that we're still not at the point where we can instantly control our brains with this knowledge - and because thousands of chemicals in the brain and body interact to determine how we feel, it's doubtful that we ever will be.

But these chemical systems exist to promote our health - and by understanding why they work the way they do, we can use science to sculpt lifestyles that are better for our minds, bodies, and souls.

Anxiety happens in two places: the body, and the brain. The brain and body are designed to communicate with each other about threats and hardships in the environment. They do this by releasing chemical messages that contain instructions such as "quick, get ready to run from a lion," "we must be in a famine, eat all the food!" and "it seems like we're in trouble here."

In this book, we will envision your life as a car on a road. The point you're starting out from is where you are *now*. We'll look at the mechanics of your "car" (your brain and body, which are the vehicles you rely on to carry you to your destination), the "driver" of your emotions, which drive which decisions you make, and the "steering wheel" of your mind – which allows you to turn the journey of your life in any direction you want, as long as your car and your driver are in good working order.

In our final section, we will discuss drawing your own "road map" - taking pro-active control of what roads you drive and choosing your own destination, rather than simply reacting to the bumps in the road you're already on.

There are books and books and classes and classes offered on each subject we cover here – from exercises which helps you tune up your "car," to tools and exercises to help you create a happy and healthy "driver" and have good control over your "steering wheel."

I hope that readers will determine which tools offered in this book are most helpful to them, and pursue more learning and practice in those areas. The power of these tools cannot be overstated – take if from someone who has lived this battle.

The goal of this book is to give a broad overview of the role of our brains and bodies in determining where we go in life – and how you can take charge of both, to ultimately take charge of your destination.

The Science Behind Anxiety – Famine and Lions

In college, I decided that I had to study neuroscience to learn how the brain worked. In just the last couple of decades, science has grown in leaps and bounds as far as illuminating the *physical* basis of our thoughts and feelings - X protein in Y part of the brain binds with Z chemical and makes you feel happy/afraid/angry.

This is behind the explosion of medications for depression and anxiety, which can change the rate of creation and destruction of some of these chemicals.

At first I struggled with the idea that our feelings having a physical basis might make them somehow less meaningful. Our feelings are intimately suffering from any purely mental problem - they are experiencing physical responses in their brains and bodies, which evolved to help us survive. Our society's rising anxiety problem is not that people have somehow gotten more weak-willed over time - it's that our society is increasingly unlike the one we evolved to survive in.

The good news is, we *can* control the direction of our lives. But this requires something in addition to willpower: it requires understanding. It requires an understanding of how our brains and bodies work, so that we can keep moving on the road we want to be on when the engine locks up or the steering goes wonky because our automatic security system thinks it saw a lion.

This book will attempt to teach some basic concepts and techniques for maintenance of the vehicles of our lives. We'll use the metaphor of cars with drivers repeatedly to talk about the journey of life.

Feel free to skip around this book to address whatever might be most pressing in your life - but please *do* take the time read and consider all the chapters. Many may be tempted to skip over one or two because they feel like they've already got that area taken care of - but because understanding is so crucial to shaping the lives we want to have, why take the chance on missing useful information?

I know a few years ago I would have skipped right over "The Anxious Body." I was convinced then that subjects like diet and exercise weren't worth my time - after all, my problem was a *mental* problem and I was never going to have a beach body or win any athletic tournaments, so why bother with what I thought of as weight loss methods?

But I was wrong. It turned out that the root of my panic attacks was intimately linked to the state of my body - specifically my lack of physical activity - and that today, physical exercise is the best way I have of boosting my confidence and keeping my anxiety in check.

So please stick with us for the full ride as we learn more about the biochemistry of anxiety and how emotions manifest in our bodies, as well as how we can take advantage of our brains' learning processes to build the kind of brain we want to have.

survival is immediately threatened - so it takes actions that it thinks will preserve us through the next few weeks of famine and lions. In doing so it puts on hold many of the mental and physical processes for *long-term* survival.

Because the body can respond to an email from your boss in the exact same way it would respond to famine, it is extremely important for us to consciously manage our cortisol levels.

Many people in the modern world are stuck in "short-term survival mode," which leads to behaviors and choices that are not healthy for us in the long-term.

People in short-term survival mode aren't just being "irresponsible" when they make unhealthy diet choices or choose to spend their time in unproductive ways - at some level they're responding to a biochemical message that they need to focus on satisfying their needs right *now* or they might not have a future at all.

That's a biochemical message that can be changed.

When cortisol levels are low, we feel more compelled to make good choices for our long-term goals - because our body is not convinced that we need to put all our resources towards avoiding starvation in the next few weeks!

Adrenaline and Norepinephrine

If cortisol is the "stress hormone," these are the "lion" hormones. These hormones are so important to survival in the wild that there are two of them; that way if one of them fails to be released, there's a backup system.

These chemicals are released by our bodies in response to immediate threats. They are responsible for many other symptoms of stress and anxiety you might recognize: high blood pressure (gets more oxygen to your muscles so you can run from lions), high blood sugar (gets more fuel to your muscles so you can run from lions), muscle tension (get ready to run from lions, guys!), racing heart (pumps more blood so you can run from lions!), sweat (cools the body so you can run from lions!) etc..

The big problem with these two hormones in the modern world is that most things that set them off are not things we can productively run from.

For example, say you're having "lion" feelings about a meeting with your boss - sprinting away at top speed will probably not lead to a good resolution. The same goes for exams, first dates, and other modern challenges.

Worse still - not only is escaping not a good option for these challenges - but because running doesn't help, we often don't run *at all*. This leaves our bodies convinced that we haven't yet outrun the lion - and that we still need to do so.

This build-up of adrenaline is what causes the physical symptoms of panic attacks - racing heart, shortness of breath, high blood pressure, and other troubling symptoms.

I was shocked when, after visiting yet another doctor due to ongoing panic attacks, the doctor recommended exercise.

"Exercise?" I asked. "What could that have to do with anxiety? It won't solve any of the things causing my anxiety, like my grades!" The doctor's response about "burning off adrenaline" didn't make sense to me at the time.

But, desperate for a solution, I tried incorporating 20 minutes of walking uphill into my daily routine. And it helped! My panic attacks weren't gone completely, but they were much less severe.

I now understand that, although my brain understood that running from my problems wouldn't help, my body didn't. And running for any reason made it feel better!

Muscle tension

We are not using our muscles even a little bit the way they are meant to be used these days. Our muscles evolved, originally, to propel us in all of our daily tasks; to sit, stand, lie, run, jump, and climb. We do almost none of those things today.

This can be okay when our lives are pretty stress-free and we have the flexibility in our daily routine to do what makes us comfortable. But when we have lots of "run from lions" signals coming at us, we're forced to sit in a chair at least 8 hours per day, and given little incentive to run or jump or climb...well, then things get problematic.

Our brain is aware of our body's tension. This is the case even if we are not consciously aware of it. Indeed, our brains have a filter that they use to determine what information is most important to be brought to the attention of our conscious minds.[4]

In the modern environment, it almost always deems highly stimulating activities like computers, televisions, and music to be "most important."

This means we are unaware of the state of our bodies almost all the time, unless we consciously choose to make time and space to be aware of them! But our brains are *always* affected by the state of our bodies - even if we don't realize it.

Study after study has shown that we feel and act differently when our muscles are tense, our postures slouched, etc.. In fact, some studies found that people who were asked to perform tasks while maintaining slouched postures gave up more easily than those with good posture - even if they weren't aware of feeling any different![3]

But we don't know *why* we're feeling and acting that way, and may not even notice that we do unless our actions strike us as odd. The state of our muscles isn't high on our priority list of things to pay attention to in this highly stimulating technological world.

The result is that many of us could take extremely simple steps, such as standing up and walking around for five minutes, doing a few stretches to counteract the "I'm slouched and stressed" posture of office work, and generally taking conscious control of our posture - to produce staggering differences in our emotions and behaviors.

When our bodies are in the state they're supposed to be in, our whole mental state changes. It's really quite remarkable.

It took me forever to realize that the my-brain-just-won't-work-anymore block I kept getting after working for more than 20 or 30 minutes could be completely dispelled by getting up and moving around for five. That's certainly more productive than staring blankly at the screen being frustrated for 20 minutes!

I'd challenge all readers of this book to try, not just to do rote exercises because I or someone else says so - but to try to learn your own personal brain-body relationship. What physical activities make your brain work better? What *doesn't* work for you?

Neural activity

While the cells in our brain are *supposed* to be responsive to the world around us (that's how we experience and think!), some cells are more responsive than others. And too much activity, just like too little activity, can cause problems for us!

It is important to understand that there are many different *systems* in the brain - just like your car includes wiring for the alternator, the air conditioner, the radio, etc., the brain contains systems for seeing and hearing, systems for planning ahead - and systems for feeling fear when threatened.

To keep these systems separate, the brain uses many different chemical messengers, called "neurotransmitters" - and even for the same messenger, there may be many different receptors that respond to the chemical in different ways.

More than one system uses each chemical messenger - this accounts for the unpredictable side effects of psychiatric medication, which vary from person to person.

The genetic variance between people - in how different neurotransmitters are produced, broken down, and responded to by cells in the brain - also helps explain why some people have higher anxiety than others.

In some people, the system in the brain for dealing with fear and danger is genetically predisposed to be more active than others. These systems can also *become* more active in people through events such as past trauma. These events can make the brain think the world is a dangerous place so it had better be on high alert.

The combination of different genetic dispositions and different life events explains why some people (like myself) may be anxious despite having had fairly tranquil childhoods, and why some people who have trauma have more lasting anxiety responses than others.

In nature, it's good for a tribe to have people of multiple different anxiety levels - a society does best when there are some people constantly on the lookout for danger and who prepare for the worst, and others who take risks and try new things.

When times are hard, it's good to have more people on the lookout - which is why most people can have anxiety "activated" by life events. This benefit to society from diverse responses may be why there are different genetic variations within the human population when it comes to how people deal with daily life and respond to stressful events.

Medications for anxiety and depression work by affecting the inter-brain messengers that activate neurons and communicate signals between them. Common anti-anxiety medications, for example, "turn down" the overall level of communication in fear- and danger-related parts of the brain.

These can be very useful for assisting people with internal "alarm systems" that are permanently set to heightened sensitivity, or for breaking the cycle of danger signals passing between the brain and body.

The First Steps

I hope that this book is helpful to people at all stages of their anxiety journey. Whether you're just beginning to consider that you might benefit from addressing your anxiety, or have been fighting a life-long battle with it, I hope to be able to offer some perspectives and encouragement from my own experience.

There are a few things I'll say that may not be popular, but which need to be said.

My journey with anxiety has definitely been a journey of many steps. I went from generally denying that I really needed to do anything about my anxiety in my youth, to admitting I had it and trying to address it through self-help and lifestyle changes.

After a year of yoga and meditation *still* had me too anxious to have success in interpersonal relationships, I sought psychotherapy.

When, after a year of that (plus yoga and meditation) I was improving in my behavior but feeling more depressed than ever, I finally caved to my doctor's repeated recommendations that I try medication.

That changed my life.

So having done it all (well, not even remotely *all*, but having at least sampled the most popular approaches to anxiety and depression in our society), here's what I would recommend to someone who is just starting out:

Psychotherapy

This, I think, has done more to change my life than anything else. Medication was the final "piece" to the puzzle (I'll explain why that may be shortly), but after a year of psychotherapy my actions, thought processes, and feelings had changed in ways that I frankly never thought possible.

After a little over a year of psychotherapy, I had a sort of "breakthrough." I couldn't explain in words or concepts what that was, but suddenly I believed that I was capable of doing things I had never *really* felt myself capable of doing before.

The difference was such that my former roommate, who had lived with me for a year but moved away few months before my breakthrough, saw photographs of me and told me that I looked different.

My posture had changed. My expression had changed. My body was literally changing shape, gaining muscle in places it had never had muscle before. I was *confident*, and that gave me the strength to do many things that I had always wanted to do.

Of course, this was not a magic bullet. As mentioned, it took somewhat over a year of weekly therapy appointments to reach that state. And it certainly wasn't a cure-all.

I still struggle to prioritize and keep myself on track to where I want to be; but the struggle is now *so much less* than it was. Many cognitive obstacles that I didn't even realize I had have been brought to light and are now being actively addressed through therapy.

Many people I speak to who have anxiety or depression have no interest in seeing a therapist. I can understand why. In my teenage years, I also refused to see one. This may have had something to do with the fact that it was the adults in my life who wanted me to see one; I had the impression that psychotherapy was supposed to make you "normal" or "just like everyone else." And I had never admired the seemingly shallow "normal" teenagers around me.

It was concerns about my relationships that finally drove me to seek therapy myself - and to my surprise, I found that my therapist was more tolerant of my eccentricities and unique ambitions than any of the adults in my life had been growing up!

Far from telling me what was "normal," my therapist was more concerned with the hurtful effects of the people in my life who had implied that I needed to be "changed" than he was about the my eccentric behaviors, which he seemed to agree were perfectly healthy for me!

All of this is why I now recommend psychotherapy as the first-line treatment for anxiety, for those who can get it and haven't yet. There is *certainly* more than *just* therapy you can do to learn to manage the vehicle of your life - but if you haven't tried therapy yet, I highly recommend it.

A therapist is like an expert auto mechanic who takes a lot of time to get to know *your* personal vehicle, your chosen destination, and the terrain you are likely to have to cover to get there!

Lifestyle changes

Let's face it, all Americans (and all people, probably) could benefit from lifestyle changes. We've already covered a bit the ways in which our bodies are not being used the way they were made to be used.

We were made to live on diets consisting mostly of vegetables, fruits, and whole grains, with a little bit of meat mixed in; we were made to walk and run and climb; we were made to run from lions, hunt wild beasts, and eat as much as possible in times of plenty.

Even beyond what we were made for, there is the question of what we *can* do. Philosophers, martial artists, and scientists have been learning progressively more about the workings of our brains and bodies across the millennia.

We (at least as a society) now know a great deal more than any animal about what we are capable of and how to make that happen.

Yet in a society driven by animal needs combined with modern technology, we don't address either of these things very well. We don't exercise because our technology doesn't require us to, and our animal brains don't want us to expend unnecessary resources.

We don't practice conscious contemplation of our surroundings because our technology doesn't require us to, and our animal brains are more easily prompted to engage in ancient pre-programmed survival responses than scientifically proven meditations.

Of course, the good thing about being conscious entities is that we can *choose*. As discussed earlier, we do not possess infinite willpower; we can't simply change our brain's and body's habits overnight.

But by determining gradually, through science and experience, how to work with our minds, bodies, and hearts - over time we can make revolutionary change.

There have never been more tools at our disposal to get to our chosen destinations. Psychotherapy and medication are two of the most powerful tools; but yoga, meditation, diet, exercise, and social activities are *also* powerful ways to reshape our brains and shape our moods.

I started my journey to where I wanted to be by joining a weekly yoga class.

Over time, that helped me lose a great deal of my fear of exercising in public; going to class week after week and doing exercises, being encouraged to try new ones - after a certain point, my yoga instructor's encouragement and the example she lived set in.

I no longer cared whether I was sure I could do something right; I was going to try it anyway, for the experience, not the outcome.

Although I did not engage enough in yoga to experience a total life transformation, it did play a role in my eating better and gaining more muscle mass (sorely needed - we're not talking "bodybuilder" here, we're talking "I can finally sit for more than a few hours without back pain!").

Perhaps most important was the way yoga made me *feel* - as a result of its interaction with my postures, and my stress hormones.

If I had engaged more in yoga and other forms of exercise, I doubtless would have experienced even greater benefits.

Indeed, it was yoga and other forms of exercise that led to my transformation after my therapy break-through - although for me, I needed the confidence I gained through therapy to be able to commit to the necessary exercises to manage my stress hormones and build postural support muscles at a high level.

Medication

This was the toughest sell for me. I have always avoided psychoactive substances like the plague. Even the prospect of alcohol creeped me out - I didn't like the thought of not being in control of my brain.

This extended not just to psychiatric medications, but to other medicines as well - when I began gaining weight in my teens, I repeatedly declined testing for hypothyroidism because I was convinced that I was "fine."

Finally after developing medical symptoms that alarmed my doctors, I was tested, and sure enough - my immune system hated my thyroid gland, and my whole body had been running on a deficit of thyroid (which basically determines how fast your metabolism functions) for who-knows-how-long.

My story with antidepressants was similar. For years I declined to use them because I was "fine" - I was higher-functioning professionally and academically than many people I knew, and I didn't *feel* depressed.

But in my mid-20s, when I began to be distressed enough about my lack of career and social progress to seek therapy, I was starting to *feel* depressed.

And when, after a year of yoga classes and therapy, I woke up one day feeling more depressed than I had ever felt before - I knew it was time for a change. Reluctantly, I went to my doctor and agreed to try an antidepressant.

In hindsight, I really should have seen that coming. As mentioned before, our responses to stress are determined by a combination of genes and environment: my family had a long history of antidepressant use, which I was convinced should not apply to me since I had a tranquil and happy childhood.

It turns out that despite my own fortunate childhood, I may still have been feeling some of the effects of hardships past. Through something called "epigenetics," a parents' experiences can actually switch on and off genes in their sperm and eggs.

This is probably yet one more way of nature allowing us to transmit useful information about our environment, and how best to respond to it. In lab mice, the offspring of happy mice actually behave differently and have different gene expression from the offspring of stressed mice![5]

This effect is not strong enough to cancel out the importance of one's own experiences; the trauma or tranquility of one's own childhood has a much stronger effect on neural development than the epigenetics one inherits.

But all of these factors - what permanent genetic variants, what epigenetic activations, what life events one experiences, and what mood-managing techniques one learns and uses - add up to determine how we respond to our environment.

So my parents' experiences could be one factor explaining why, although I'd had a fairly tranquil and prosperous childhood, I'd shown symptoms of anxiety from an early age.

Medication turned out to be the last missing piece to the puzzle of why I couldn't seem to take charge of my life. Though most people don't feel the effects of antidepressants for four to six weeks, I felt the effects of a low dose within a few days. Within a few days, I felt the way I was *supposed* to feel.

It came with some odd side effects - for those first few days, I had symptoms of panic attacks at the drop of a hat. I also woke up a lot in the middle of the night, sometimes in a panic.

But these effects soon diminished, and the trade-off was worth it. I now had the kind of energy I had always envied in other people; the energy to get up in the morning and do things!

Of course, different medicines will be right for different people. Some people have a type of depression that manifests as anxiety, and so will be helped by anti-depressants; others may have just straightforward anxiety, which is helped by other types of medications.

And medication may not be appropriate for you at all, if your anxiety does stem primarily from lifestyle choices (which can include caffeine consumption, incessant technology use, a very sedentary lifestyle, etc.) or thought patterns.

It is also important to note that people may respond differently to the same medications. For me, my doctors had a pretty good idea of where to start - on the medication that several of my blood relatives had responded well to. And the result was fantastic - far from feeling "numbed" or "zombie-like" as I had heard some people characterize the effects of anti-depressants, I felt like myself, just with more energy and less stress.

Others may need to try a few medications before they find the one that's right for them. Today, there are dozens of choices of medications that change brain chemistry in different ways, and may work best for people with different genetic profiles.

So for all that it's often demonized as a "quick fix" or "really just a placebo," medication is one more tool in our arsenal to combat the effects of past trauma. In combination with therapy and a healthy lifestyle - well, I think my testimony speaks for itself.

Now that I've gotten to explain what I see as the most important tools for fighting anxiety and depression (and yes, two out of three of these are things this book can't give you), onto what this book *can* give you - the science to understand, and some tips for implementing small activities each day that can help you on the road to your chosen destination.

Chapter 2: The Anxious Body / The Wheels on the Bus

To some degree, it is obvious that it is our body that is responsible for taking us where we want to go. If our heart stops beating, we're obviously not in good shape.

But the importance of having our body in good working order when it comes to our *state of mind* is widely overlooked by modern Western culture. For centuries, our scholars have rejected the idea that our minds *arise* from our bodies – in the words of one of my neuroscience professors: "The mind is what the body does."

Eastern culture, which never developed this idea of the mind and body as being two completely separate and unrelated entities, have developed and maintained across the millennia *physical* practices which were designed to optimize one's state of *mind*, such as yoga, tai chi, and indeed most martial arts.

When I was growing up, I was sure that physical exercise was not for me. It took time, it took effort, and I simply didn't believe that it really affected the state of my mind. My mind was my priority: my body could wait.

Only after enduring many years of mental blocks I could not explain, which prevented me from getting where I wanted to be in life – I wanted to be a published writer – did I cave in and seriously begin examining physical conditioning as a means of improving my mental state.

And, well, you can see the evidence right here – now I am where I wanted to be. I am a professional writer.

So in this chapter, we'll take a long, honest look at how modern culture can pose problems for the very mechanics of our "bus" – the physical chemistry of our brains and bodies. And how we can learn to fix those mechanical problems, and even turbo-charge our ride through life!

The Wrong Attitude Towards Exercise

The body is the often-overlooked root of our minds.

Eastern philosophers have always taught that the mind and body are one, manifesting this belief through spiritual practices that also conditioned the body, such as yoga, tai chi, meditation, and karate. However, Western philosophers have taken a different view for millennia - resulting in some of the problems of Western culture today.

The philosophy that spread throughout Europe through the Roman Empires was one in which the body and soul were inherently separate - and the body was the inferior of the two. The mind, or soul, was a being of pure thought which was only temporarily inconvenienced by having a physical body; and the physical body was mostly a source of limitation and temptation.

For centuries, then, the greatest virtue in Western thought was to "rise above" the body by ignoring it to the triumph of the mind.

Plato – arguably the founder of Western thought as we know it – taught that the soul and body belonged to entirely different realms and were made of entirely different materials. That, in fact, is the root of the word "platonic" - which means "transcending physical desires."

To Plato and his students, the highest pursuits were those which were strictly mental. This was happily embraced by the Church of the Middle Ages, which saw the non-physical soul as the only important part of a person, while it saw the body almost exclusively as a source of temptations to sin which must be overcome by sheer willpower.

This attitude that "thinking good thoughts" is merely a matter of willpower lingers in our society to this day. It is also a major factor behind the stigmatization of mental illness – if the mind is an independent entity, separate from the body, surely any problems with the mind arise from the mind itself.

This explains the widespread lack of understanding of mental illness - if the mind is a being of pure thought, independent of the physical body, surely there cannot be such a thing as mental illness the same way there is physical illness!

This attitude, unfortunately, ignores basically everything we know about medical science. Informed by a century of neuroscience, we now know that our minds, or at least what we can perceive of them in this life, arise from physical processes which are susceptible to physical disease and dysfunction just like our other organs.

And just like with our other organs, what we put into our minds - and what mental "muscles" we exercise - determine how well our minds function.

Only in recent years has science truly begun to understand how our brains and bodies exchange chemical signals to tell us how much stress we're under and how we should act. And only *very* recently have scientists begun to understand the full impact of the fact that most people in Western societies have very little incentive or encouragement to exercise our bodies.

It turns out that lack of exercise severely impacts our neurological development, and may be a direct cause of increasing frequency of mental illness in our population.

Indeed, since the popularization of the Internet over outdoor play and the decrease in recess in schools, neurologists have become increasingly alarmed over the connection between lack of physical activity and poor academic performance, poor neuromuscular development, and psychiatric problems in young people.[6]

I know I grew up with the attitude that the body was inconsequential to the mind. For many years, since I did not believe I could (nor did I particularly want to) become a competitive athlete, I felt that there was no point in exercising or conditioning my body.

Surely, I thought, those folks who said they felt better when they exercised just meant that they felt like they *looked* better to other people.

I didn't feel that a beach body or social recognition for athletics were within my reach, so I didn't think I had anything to gain from exercising. If anything, the monotonous repetitive motions sounded like a waste of my valuable time – which I needed to do other things, such as manage my anxiety.

But it turns out you don't have to change anything about your appearance or your athletic skill to feel better from exercising.

It turns out that physical activity is a powerful way of regulating stress hormones – the hormones that your body releases when it encounters daily stresses, such as deadlines or exams, and interprets those to mean that you're being chased by a lion. Physical exercise also increases the metabolism and overall health of brain cells!

I would not understand *why* exercise can make us feel better until I was most of the way through my Neuroscience degree in college. But I did discover that physical activity could profoundly improve my mental state when I discovered yoga in high school.

Back then, I would never have signed up for a yoga class. Yoga was exercise, and exercise was something that I wasn't any good at and that wasn't worth my time, anyway. Yoga also wasn't included in my gym classes, which focused almost entirely on competitive tasks like sports and running laps on a timer (which I naturally hated, because I always came in last).

I was fortunate enough, however, to have a speech teacher who used yoga exercises to help prepare students to express their emotions. Speech was a required class in my high school, so there was no getting out of it – and even though I abhorred the part where I had to "perform" speeches, I was shocked to discover that the part yoga made me feel *good*.

Part of that was probably due to the fact that yoga is specifically formulated as a *spiritual* practice – yogis in India practice, not because they want beach bodies or athletic trophies, but because they want inner peace and clarity. It's not something that's inherently competitive, or measures its progress based on outside measures like how much weight you can lift.

The fact that that's so confusing to us Westerners is a testament to our mindset – the idea that a *physical* activity would be undertaken for *mental/emotional* benefits is alien to us, while to an Easterner, it's perfectly natural, because the Eastern religions always saw the mind and body as unified, cooperative forces - not separate forces that compete for our time and energy.

A major part of why yoga worked for me when nothing else had is simply that it was not done in a competitive setting. In school, or even in adult life, when are we encouraged to exercise? In group classes and team sports, in the context of "losing weight" or preparing for some competitive test of athletic prowess.

Even Westernized yoga classes often fall prey to this - in my own thoroughly spiritual, anti-competitive class, I heard horror stories from other trainees of yoga studios where they had been pressured or ridiculed for "failing to conform." If that ever happens to you in a yoga class, find a different one - they are not *supposed* to be like that!

Growing up in this Western culture, where exercise is only to look good - no wonder I, who was overweight from an early age and socially awkward besides, had no interest exercising at all. As one critic recently observed, Westerners think of exercise only in terms of competition – if it can't be counted and compared, then we see no point in doing it.

Even our practitioners of yoga, who may talk about the mental and spiritual benefits of their exercise routine, tend to measure their "progress" by how long they can hold a pose, or how far they can stretch.

To an Eastern yogi, it does make sense to pursue progress – but progressing poses and endurance are regarded as outward signs of *inward* growth - of, in fact, growth of the brain and body mechanisms of regulating mood.

Westerners are in constant danger of developing the opposite attitude – that the reason for cultivating mental discipline and peace through yoga is simply to allow us to get thinner and perform more impressive physical feats.

This is a very dangerous attitude. Can you imagine if physicians implied that the main reason to take antibiotics was to lose weight and impress your friends? Most Americans wouldn't bother to take them, and many would take them for completely the wrong reasons!

If we view the mental discipline and spiritual well-being that comes with exercise as mere tools to the end of impressing others, no wonder more of us aren't doing it. No wonder people like me can even find ourselves looking *down* on those who exercise as being motivated by superficial desires.

I certainly never would have started exercising if I'd thought that the main reason to exercise was to look better or even to improve my physical health. Besides thinking those things were out of my reach, they just weren't anywhere close to the top of my priority list.

An Eastern yogi, of course, would say that the reasons for exercising are deep, spiritual, and profound – that physical strength and conditioning are mere side effects of practices which improve the state of our mind and our spiritual understanding.

An Eastern yogi would say that we exercise like we take antibiotics – not so that other people can watch us take them or so we can talk about it at social events, but so that we'll feel better.

This does not just apply to yoga. Indeed, as I learned later in life, some of the same mental and emotional benefits can be gained from any form of exercise.

Yoga certainly had its unique strengths for me – it does address the body and mind more comprehensively than simple squats or push-ups. But those exercises which are usually regarded as means to superficial ends have enough important things in common with yoga to make them worthwhile.

I came into adulthood with weak muscles; although I still have no ambition to enter weight-lifting contests, having stronger core muscles has caused by body to communicate more confidence in my abilities to my mind.

I came into adulthood with no exercise practice; although I don't expect to *ever* run a marathon, I now exercise because doing so decreases the stress signals I get from my muscles and makes me feel better when I wake up in the morning.

Any form of exercise that gets the muscles moving and the blood pumping will help to "burn off" adrenaline, release stress tension, and generally change body chemistry to promote higher mood and clearer thinking.

The Wheels on the Bus: Meeting the Brain's Physical Needs

Exercise is the biggest thing that most of us are lacking as far as meeting our brain's needs. We're usually pretty good at eating *some* nutrients, drinking *some* water, getting *some* sleep, etc.. But in our modern world, many adults get almost no physical exercise.

Yet *all* of these things are physical necessities for the proper functioning of our brains - and all of them are in some way impaired in our modern culture. Here are some changes you can make when you're ready to improve your brain health, and your overall well-being:

Exercise

Any kind of exercise is better than none.

Walking, jogging, squats, sit-ups, and push-ups are easy ways to exercise at home.

Above and beyond that full mind-body practices such as yoga and tai chi work to reduce anxiety by training us to be conscious of many aspects of our mind-body relationship.

Cut out soda. Seriously.

It's not just about weight loss - caffeine can be a major contributor to anxiety and other mental health symptoms, even triggering panic attacks and other psychiatric symptoms in some people[7] (I am one such person).

While the occasional pick-me-up probably won't hurt, drinking caffeine every day can significantly contribute to anxiety, insomnia, and even urinary tract infections.

If that weren't enough, soda in particular has the twin evils of high sugar and carbonic acid (a necessary byproduct of carbonation) - both of which are leading causes of tooth decay. The acid *literally* eats away at your teeth, and the sugar feeds bacteria which make more acid.

This has led to the dental nickname "Mountain Dew mouth" – for people who show up with large amounts of severe cavities after habitually drinking large amounts of soda[8].

It also goes without saying that the massive amounts of sugar in soda add up to increased body fat and high blood sugar - risks for cardiovascular disease and diabetes.

Try *these* instead:

Water. When you're thirsty, your brain wants water first and foremost. Think of it as being like the oil for your engine. Putting water into your body without adding extra sugar, acid, or fat is ideal.

Of course, there are also other drinks that can be good for your health in moderation, such as…

Fruit juice. You still get the blood sugar pick-me-up, but no caffeine, less acid, and more vitamins and minerals.

Coffee. You still get caffeine and acid (too much caffeine for sensitive folks like me to do well with regular coffee, in fact), but no sugar and more beneficial antioxidants. Coffee has some of the same risks as soda - high caffeine and acid content. But in moderation it's better for you than its artificially flavored, sugary cousin.

Tea. Like coffee, it's a touch acidic and contains caffeine - but it contains less caffeine than coffee, so you'd have to consume more for it to be a problem. Tea also contains beneficial antioxidants. In addition to "true" teas from the tea plant, herbal teas such as mint, chamomile, and others generally contain no caffeine and may contain other beneficial compounds from plants.

Skim milk drinks. Skim milk contains protein, calcium, and vitamin D - three important ingredients for your health. Protein is especially useful as a source of long-term energy that won't spike your blood sugar. However, beware full-fat milk, as it drastically increases calorie count and saturated animal fats may contribute to the risk of cardiovascular disease.

Soy, almond, and coconut milks. I'll confess, I'm a sucker for these guys. They're often fortified with more calcium and vitamin D than milk, and confer their own unique health benefits. Soy milk has more protein than cow's milk, for example, and almond milk contains fewer calories. Coconut milk contains saturated fats - but of a sort of plant-based saturated fat that is metabolized differently by the body, potentially leading to higher good cholesterol.

Nutrition

If water is the oil for your engine, food is the fuel. Very few folks in our modern culture have a truly healthy relationship with food. Due to our harried lifestyle, some do a lot of stress eating - others may forget to eat regularly at all.

Both can contribute to our brain feeling wired and anxious. Here are some quick ways you can ensure that you eat regularly throughout the day, and help yourself avoid the desire to binge eat:

Trail mix. A combination of nuts, dried fruit, and chocolate bits if you must (I must), will give your body nutrition that is far more filling than empty carbohydrates. Trail mix *is* a high calorie food, and sometimes a high-cholesterol food depending on what types of nuts you use (you may wish to read up on the nutritional information of nuts before making your own blend)

But by supplying protein, fiber, fat, vitamins, and minerals in a mobile form, it can help you remember to eat every few hours and potentially avoid binge eating as a result of extreme hunger later. Try measuring out reasonable portions of trail mix to eat at scheduled snack breaks throughout the day.

Granola bars – Dozens of companies make granola bars pre-packaged for your enjoyment – but I'm rather fond of making my own. Peanut butter and nutella can be mixed with honey to provide a firm binding agent; nuts can supply protein, chia and flax seeds brain-healthy omega threes, dried fruits and whole oats fiber and complex carbs, and bits of chocolate can give you a little more incentive to eat.

Savory seeds – Nuts, pumpkin seeds, and toasted corn are among savory snacks that come in a variety of sweet and savory flavors – along with complex carbs and fiber to keep you going longer than potato chips or cookies.

Sleep! Eight hours per day is important! In these days where shift work and irregular schedules are increasingly common, it can be especially difficult to establish a healthy sleep schedule. However, it is well-documented that getting enough sleep is important for learning, memory, mood, and judgment. During sleep, the brain and body perform several important functions that don't happen during the waking hours. Among other benefits:

Learning and memory are consolidated. In fact, studies have found that mice who get sufficient REM sleep learn faster and remember better than those who have been sleep-deprived.[9]

Stress hormone levels are lowered, and immune function is increased. The body produces more antibodies during sleep than it does during waking.[10]

Sleep deprivation leads to mood swings and impaired judgment; in fact in many states it is illegal to drive if you haven't slept in 24 hours, because that is effectively the same as driving drunk![11]

Chapter 3: The Anxious Heart - The Driver

It may seem odd to some that I am treating the mind and emotions separately in this book, and that I have designated emotions – not the mind – as the "driver."

But there's a very good reason for this. As discussed in the previous chapter, thought is in fact a *physical* process. It is a process that is affected by our will, but also by physical factors which have little to do with objective truth – for example, our emotional state can actually drastically change our perception of the world.

The same situation can look hopeless and insurmountable, or challenging but completely doable – depending on our emotional state.

From an evolutionary perspective, our emotions are part of how our brain produces the best possible response to our environment. The problem is, this response system was designed for an environment completely different from the one in which we now live (unless, you know, you're an African hunter-gatherer with a Kindle). So the emotional calculations that tell us when a situation can be overcome and when we're better off not even trying – do not work at all for our modern world.

This is the root of much hopelessness and "learned helplessness" – a well-studied phenomenon seen in lab animals in psychology, where even if what the animals want is easily within their reach, they will not reach out and take it – because past bad experiences have convinced them that doing so is impossible, or not worthwhile.

What have you always wanted that is within your grasp now? What might you not be reaching for because your emotions are telling you – incorrectly – that it's impossible.

You'll have a better idea of what lies within your grasp when you know how to handle the "driver" of your car – your emotions.

When you recognize external factors that can affect your emotions – quite irrationally, and often in a negative direction – and tools which you can use to affect your emotions in a *positive* direction – you will have much more power to reach for what you want that may already be within your grasp.

So in this chapter, we have an exploration of what emotions are, where they come from – and how you can manage emotions that were made to operate in small hunter-gatherer tribes on the African savannah, in a healthy and conscious way in the modern world.

What is Emotion, Really?

On the face of it, this may seem a silly question. "Of course we know what emotion is - we live with it every day of our lives!"

But in fact, there is a very important truth about emotion that often goes unrecognized: emotion lives in the body.

We are accustomed to thinking of emotion as a *mental* state with *mental* causes. "I am sad because X happened," or "I am scared because I don't want Y to happen." We are accustomed to the idea that emotion is at least somewhat logical.

That's *half* right - emotions are ultimately caused by signals that the brain sends to the body. However, what we perceive as emotion is often a *physical* sensation - and the brain can read physical conditions, such as slouched posture, as emotional states as well.

Think about what you *feel* when you are experiencing an emotion. Perhaps you are hot with embarrassment, or warm with pleasure. Perhaps you are cold with fear, or your palms are sweating. Perhaps you feel sadness as an ache in your chest, or joy as a thrill of energy through your body. Perhaps you feel butterflies in your stomach or your heart is racing with excitement.

Many of these sensations are caused by the brain sending signals to the body - but ultimately, what we perceive as emotion lives in the *physical* body - not just in the realm of our thoughts. In fact, sometimes emotion may be caused by the sensations in our bodies - even if we think they are caused for a logical reason!

Studies with "split brain" patients - patients whose brain hemispheres have been surgically separated as a treatment for severe epilepsy - show that we can concoct stories to give a rational explanation for why we feel the way we do - even if we don't *really* know the reason for our feeling.

To learn this, scientists showed split-brain patients different pictures that only one side of the brain could see, since the surgery had made it impossible for the eye to communicate internally to both sides of the brain.

When the right brain was shown a funny picture, the right brain would send signals to the body, telling it to laugh. But when asked *why* they were laughing, the patient's left brain would make up a story - "I was thinking about something funny that happened earlier."

The left brain didn't know anything about the funny picture that the right brain had been shown - but it reacted to the laugh by making up a logical story to explain why it was laughing!

This is a reflection of how the state of our bodies can affect our emotions. Are we *really* feeling down because life is bleak, or are we feeling down because we have muscle pain we have not acknowledged and addressed? Are we angry at society because life is terribly unfair, or is it because we have lots of fight-or-flight adrenaline built up that we haven't burned off?

Of course, none of this conversation is meant to minimize the importance of emotions to our experience of life.

Emotions are, after all, the very fabric of our being and experience - and this is the very reason why it is so important to understand where they come from, and how we can work with them to shape the self and experience that we want to have!

In this chapter, instead of focusing on the sweeping generalizations about what we can do to improve the "body" side of our constant mind-body dialogue, we will examine some specific ways to shape this dialogue to produce the emotions we want to have.

We will also attempt to shed some light on the exquisite dance between honoring one's emotions, and being ruled by them.

Emotion as Your Life Partner

The "exquisite dance" we do with our emotions is this - to neither neglect them, nor be ruled by them. You have probably done both at some point in your life.

Think about it - when have you felt helpless to achieve your goals, because they just seemed too hopeless to even begin to take the first step? When have you attempted to ignore something that you secretly knew you felt, because it wasn't convenient?

It may surprise the reader to know that these two things are often two sides of the same coin. Being enslaved by one emotion often leads to ignoring other feelings - when one feels hopeless or afraid for example, it may be easiest to ignore any desire for something better because achieving it may feel impossible.

Likewise, ignoring emotions instead of using them to take action towards what you really want can lead to a build-up that eventually becomes impossible to manage in a productive way.

Both potential missteps can be seen everywhere in our culture. How often do you hear someone saying that they "couldn't" do something because their emotions were too strong - or cautioning you against heeding your emotions, because that could be dangerous?

I find it helpful to think of emotions as a useful partner – as with any friend or lover, you want to value what they are saying and learn from what they can teach you – but you do *not* want to let them rule you.

Ask yourself: if my emotions were a person, would I be behaving respectfully towards them right now? Would I be according them the value they deserve in our relationship? Would I be taking the time to listen to them? Would I be recognizing their strengths?

Likewise; if my emotions were a person, would I be letting them rule my life? Are they telling me what to do to the point that I feel powerless? Why is that happening? Why am I not able to stop them from pushing me around? Do I need counseling due to a toxic relationship with my emotions, just like toxic relationships need couples' counseling?

One of the biggest mistakes we often make managing our emotions is treating them as bad things. I almost did that right in this sentence - I almost said "dealing with" instead of "managing," as though my emotions were necessary evils rather than useful members of the "team" of my existence.

When we feel anxious, or angry, or afraid, the first response Western society teaches us to have is to look for someone to blame. "You are feeling bad," it says, "so someone must have done something wrong." Negative emotions are, in our minds, things that are never supposed to happen - not useful sources of information about our world.

Some of us may instantly look outside ourselves for an object of blame, be it our boss, our teacher, our society in general, or just whoever happens to be closest to us at the time. Others among us may blame ourselves: "clearly there's something wrong with *me* because I'm angry, or sad, or afraid."

This view that negative emotions always mean that something is bad, and that we or someone else must be to blame, encourages us to either ignore or be ruled by our emotions. If we blame ourselves, we try to pretend our emotions don't exist - if we blame others, we fall into the trap of believing that we have no choice in how to feel about other people's actions.

But what if negative emotions weren't always a bad thing? What if they could be useful sources of information about who we are, and what we can do to create the lives we want to have?

With the Western mindset that everyone "should" be happy and that anything less implies that someone has done something wrong, it's easy for negative emotions to become a vicious cycle.

"I am sad, so I'm angry with myself for being sad, so I'm sad because I'm angry with myself..." or "I am angry with this person because they made me angry, so they are angry with me, so I am angry at them..."

Simply forcing ourselves to stop being scared or sad or angry doesn't work, either. It's like trying to dam up a river that just keeps flowing: eventually, the dam will overflow. And when it does, you've got a big problem on your hands, especially if you started doing something in the river's path that's now going to be destroyed by the outpouring of how you truly feel.

How, then, are we to manage our emotions in a positive way?

Try this checklist the next time you realize you are experiencing a negative emotion:

Stop. How do you feel right now? Examine the sensations in your body. What emotions

want to be heard?

Take a breath. If you are able, take several breaths to get air flowing to and from your belly. Tell your emotions it is going to be alright. You'll deal with this.

Why are you angry, sad, or afraid? The words that come to you now, after a moment of truly *feeling* your feelings and reflecting on them, may be very different and more enlightening than those that would have come in the moment of immediate reaction. This allows you to communicate better with others *and* yourself about what actions - by others, or yourself - are hurting you.

If you are facing someone who has made you sad, angry, or afraid, or someone who may be able to help - **tell them** what you have discovered in your moment of reflection. If you are alone, write it in a journal instead. You will almost certainly learn more as you write and talk.

The goal of the method stated above is not to *stop* your feelings. It is not to "make them go away," or make them disappear. Feelings are the colorful carriers of information about our world and our place in it.

Negative feelings recur for a few reasons. Like all things, our propensity to feel them is a combination of our genes and environment.

Sometimes, due to genetics or past trauma, our brains may be programmed to be so sensitive to negative emotions, or so slow to make positive ones, that we may need the help of medication to reverse some of the effects of past or present trauma on our brains.

But other times, negative feelings may recur because we have not yet acted on the useful information they contain in a way that deeply satisfies us.

Perhaps, with our reflexes of wanting to ignore our feelings, make them go away, or blame ourselves or someone else for their very existence, we may not have even discovered what useful information they carry with our conscious minds.

To this day, I struggle with profound anger at the religion I was raised in - after having been told all my life that this religion was "the only way to perfect good," I observed more and more instances of its members being hypocritical and outright cruel as I got older.

For many years after I finally publicly disavowed the religion, I had no idea how to interact with its members. A tiny - or even imagined - look of disapproval could send me into an internal paroxysm of rage.

Which I bottled up inside me, not wanting to "make waves," or make people uncomfortable," until it became too much to control. Then, the dam would break all at once - and you can just about imagine how pretty that was. By avoiding "making other people uncomfortable," I was making them a lot more uncomfortable in the end.

My expressions of anger were treated by those around me as a moral failing - as something that should not exist. My anger was treated as something that was wrong, that should not exist. I was told that, to be virtuous, I should not have anger at all.

This did precisely nothing to stop me from having it.

It was somewhat of an epiphany when, under the guidance of my therapist, I was able to see my anger as something new. It was not a sign of some moral failing or illness: it was a sign of something that was *important* to me.

Social justice, it turned out, was incredibly important to me - and I felt betrayed by my church, which had claimed to be the ultimate agent of social justice but which often seemed to actively attack people who were already marginalized and hurting.

This very important piece of information was transformative - and not just for me.

In time, I was able to articulate clearly just *why* I was angry. What behaviors it was that pissed me off - it could be as subtle as an unspoken implication that non-members of our church were not as good as church members, were in some essential way inferior to them.

As I grew to be more able to articulate the source of this terrible feeling of rage, I was able to do things to alleviate it in myself. I was able talk to the people who behaved hurtfully and be honest with them about the effects of their actions; I was able to create writing and art which expressed the feelings of those groups that were so marginalized, and portrayed their beauty.

Realizing why I was so angry and that others must feel just as angry as me, I was able to make gifts for those people as well as for myself.

I was also able to confront others with the *truly* bad things that had been done by them or their friends - I could confront them when they said things that were demeaning or victim-blaming towards others, could tell them exactly *why* I had a problem with their attitudes.

More than one person, upon being confronted with my perception of their actions and words, apologized and admitted to having used their religion to defend their own deeply flawed prejudices.

I use this example, not because it is the only time I have wrestled with awareness of my feelings, but because it was the time in which the most remarkable change was most clearly visible to me.

What information could you learn from your own most intense negative feelings?

How could they help teach you what you need - both in terms of comfort measures and self-compassion, and in terms of action and change in your life?

Speaking of comfort measures - here are some things you may not know about that have powerful effects on brain and body chemistry, which may be useful to you in getting to where you want to go:

Aromatherapy – A Matter of Chemistry

Scents have profound power to change our physical and mental states. Very early in our evolutionary history, our brains learned to respond differently to different scent compounds. Some scents meant wonderful things, like calorie-rich food or attractive mates – others meant terrible things, like disease or predators.

By exposing our brains to chosen scents, we can influence our entire brain-body state. With the growing popularity of essential oils, scientists have been studying the effects of plant-based scents with fascinating results.

Some have been found to be directly beneficial to anxiety and depression; others have been found to soothe physical aches and pains, or boost energy levels and reduce errors.

To use an essential oil for aromatherapy, add just 2-3 drops to a diffuser for a delicate scent that spreads throughout the room. Diffusers are sold online in many shapes and forms, and can also be made at home using common ingredients such as jars and bowls, tissues and paper towels, and jar lids or plates to control the flow of air and the release of scent.

***Safety warning:** All of the essential oils discussed here are intended for aromatherapy use. Though some "health" sites will tell you to put these directly on your skin, or even in your food, DO NOT DO THAT. Experienced aromatherapists advise against using even lavender oil undiluted, and know that drinking a drop of peppermint oil is like drinking 30 cups of mint tea!

A single drop of essential oil contains the bioactive compounds from many plants, and should not be applied to the skin or ingested unless safely diluted.

Several of these oils can be used as ingredients in skin lotions or foods, but please do extensive research before using them for these purposes, as even some well-established health sites do not take into account the possible side effects of ingesting concentrated plant oils or spreading them on your skin.

All that being said, like any household chemical, these can make our lives a lot better when used properly. Here are my personal favorite essential oils for aromatherapy:

Lemon - The scent of lemon oil powerfully relaxes and clarifies the mind. These effects are so powerful that offices and factories in Japan routinely scent their offices with lemon essential oil because this scent measurably increases efficiency and decreases error rates. And it's not just about being more productive – lemon essential oil is my personal favorite scent because it profoundly relaxes me, which is probably how it accomplishes those other feats.

Orange - The scent of orange essential oil has been found to have similar relaxing qualities to lemon – but this sweeter, more acutely pleasurable scent is at its best when it is relaxing and uplifting the mood. The aromatherapy benefits of orange essential oil have been used to treat people with anxiety and depression following chemotherapy, and have even been used to lower stress-related high blood pressure. I am fond of carrying a bottle of orange or lemon essential oil in my pocket, in case I need a few quick sniffs throughout the day!

Peppermint - The scent of peppermint oil, like the scent of orange and lemon oil, has been found to be relaxing and uplifting. But the scent of peppermint oil also has other benefits – it seems to soothe the pain circuits that are involved in headaches and nausea, making it an ideal relaxant when you are feeling physically stressed, ill, or in pain.

Lavender - The scent of lavender oil is one of the most effective natural sleep aids there is. I once accidentally used the same diffuser I'd used for lavender oil to try to wake me up with lemon oil in the morning – this did not work as well as planned!

In addition to guiding the brain towards sound sleep, lavender oil profoundly relaxes the mind and body, and may even reduce muscular aches and pains!

Try scheduling a five-minute aromatherapy break, as needed, to consciously manage the state of your body and mind.

Music Changes Brain Activity

In this digital age, we all use music. iPods and other devices put music at our fingertips, no matter where we are or where we're going. But do we use it mindfully?

We all know that music affects the way we feel - it can be powerfully energizing, relaxing, or cathartic. It can soothe and calm us, rev us up, remind us of what's really important - or it can merely be a distraction from our thoughts and surroundings.

Which way do you use it?

I have noticed some interesting things about my relationship with music. As a child, I preferred what we would these days term "meditation music" - music with a slower tempo and slowly evolving, thoughtful melody.

As I grew older, what I looked for in my music changed - I tended, like much of our culture, towards frenetic beats and complicated instrumental arrangements - I looked for things that would energy me or at least do a thorough job of distracting me from my daily commute.

But what is the ideal balance between these musical types? Could the addition of some music designed to slow the breath and relax the mind help me be more mindful - even if my initial craving is for something that matches my hyped-up mood?

Scientific studies on the effects of music have yielded staggering results. Rather than producing a small change, like the sounds of everyday life, the art of music can change our whole brain's activation patterns.

When looking at musicians and listeners under functional MRI machines that measure brain activity, scientists found that listening to jazz created the same creative, uninhibited brain activation patterns in listeners as in the musicians who played the music!

A separate study found that singing the same song can synchronize people's brain waves - and that people who sing together form deep, long-lasting social bonds faster than those who socialize in other ways.

A test of gene expression showed that classical music increased the expression of genes that promote learning, and decreased the expression of genes related to brain cell death and dementia.

In summary, a variety of different kinds of music seem to affect our brain in different ways. As with other pieces of technology, then, we can benefit from using music consciously to produce the types of lives we want to live.

One interesting recent development in music has been the advent of "binaural beats." This style of music, which was impossible before the advent of headphones, feeds slightly different sounds to each ear, and claims in that way to be able to affect brain activity in more specific ways than other genres of music.

Producers of binaural beats claim that their products will encourage certain types of brainwave activity - such as "alpha waves," which characterize a conscious but relaxed state of mind, gamma waves, which may be associated with the same benefits as transcendental meditation, and delta waves, which assist with sleep.

Studies of the truth of these claims have had mixed results - scientists have found that some binaural beats can create the effects they claim to have, but not all music on the market claiming to be "binaural" may do this successfully.

As with any relaxation or meditation technique, the best measure of how well it works for you is your own experience. If you are struggling with conscious relaxation, meditation, or sleep, perhaps give binaural beats a try.

I have been impressed with the effect of binaural beats on my meditation practice - but as with essential oils, use this music only as directed! My roommate once tried to sleep with alpha wave music playing and ended up having quite a negative experience, as his brain was apparently confused by the combination of brain waves it had going on!

So next time you're facing a jog, bus ride, or other listening session - ask yourself a few questions:

Could I benefit from meditation during this session? What sorts of music would be helpful to that?

How do I want to feel at the end of this listening session? Do I want to feel empowered or relaxed?

Is it possible that it might be good for me to go a while without music - listening to my surroundings, such as silence or my neighbors?

Mindfulness – The Difference Between Creation and Destruction

Throughout history, there have been arguments about the pros and cons of new technologies.

Perhaps no technology has been alternately glorified and demonized than the Internet - which optimists claimed would unite the world into one peaceful, global village, and make us all more informed citizens, while pessimists suggested it would allow evil influences to reach right into our bedrooms and seduce us away from the good.

There's a reason that all technology has been viewed as a double-edged sword - it's because technology *is* a double-edged sword. Technology empowers us; and power can produce great good when used wisely - or great evil when used unwisely.

In the case of the Internet, what we see in the real world is a mixed bag. Colleges offer online courses for free that people can take right in their own homes; artists and scientists collaborate from across the world, even allowing ordinary people to partake in new discoveries and works of art.

People in countries across the globe can now talk to each other directly, dispelling much of the power of propaganda and making it harder for governments to cover up their misdeeds.

But, on the flip side - we are all getting more anxious. Worse still, fear and anxiety often translate into hostile behavior - thus explaining the Internet phrase "don't read the comments," and the rash of cyberbullying and vitriol in partisan politics in online forums.

Why should this be so?

The most important factor, in my opinion, is the way in which the Internet interacts with our ancient survival instincts.

This interaction is something that no one saw coming, and something which scientists are only just beginning to understand. Understanding how the Internet affects us, it turns out, is also very important to understanding all sorts of self-destructive behaviors!

To understand how technology affects us - and how to use it mindfully - we must understand how the brain decides what it wants us to do.

What's Addictive Is Not Rewarding

Historically, it has been assumed that the "pleasure center" of the brain was responsible for driving our behavior. If something felt good, the logic went, we would do it more. If something felt bad, we wouldn't do it more. That seems logical, right?

The only problem is, it turns out this view is completely wrong. Recent advances in neuroscience have revealed that the brain's "pleasure center," which lights up when something feels good, and its "motivation center," which makes us want to do things more, are two completely separate entities.[13]

Upon thinking about evolution a little bit harder, this does begin to make sense - actions such as swimming to keep our heads above water, for example - one activity that activates the "motivation center" in lab mice - are not best described as "pleasurable." Indeed, it's often stress that triggers the greatest need for motivation!

It seems that our brain's motivation center cares more about seeing that we've made something happen - whether that "something" is doing a good deed whose effects spread widely, posting a vicious Internet comment that gets many replies, or hitting "refresh" on our inbox every ten seconds - than about whether what we're doing feels good.

Interestingly, this "motivation center" model also explains drug addiction far better than the "pleasure center model - surveys of drug addicts have *never* held up the idea that drug use always, or even usually, feels good.

Many addicts reported that they would do anything to get a hit even after the drug had lost all pleasurable effects - while at the same time, some drugs which were described as "extremely pleasurable" by users produced none of the classical hallmarks of addiction, such as inability to stop.

It seems, then, that our culture has been wrong for centuries about what we think spawns addiction - what makes an action dangerously addictive has little to do with how much pleasure this gives us.

This may explain why you can't stop arguing about politics online.

Because, you see, the Internet provides instant gratification. And by "gratification" I don't just mean things that may feel good - it allows us to feel like we've *done* something, instantly and over and over again.

Even if refreshing your inbox is not, realistically, advancing your career, or if arguing with strangers online is making you more depressed about the state of the world - these activities still give little hits of dopamine to the motivation center of your brain, encouraging you to waste precious time and energy on activities that *also* trigger biological stress reactions.

This potentially addictive quality of technology is especially worrisome when we look at *other* effects that technology use has on our bodies.

Emails from our bosses and hostile Internet comments, it turns out, may affect our bodies exactly the way that having a lion loose in the room would. We feel threatened - and the stress hormones flow, causing deleterious effects such as anxiety attacks, high blood pressure, and cravings for fat and sugar.

Worse still, feeling threatened can cause other negative emotions - such as hostility towards others who we feel threatened by, which might be why social media often becomes horrible and divisive instead of being a great unifying force.

I am not arguing that the Internet is *bad*. Far from it, I am an optimist when it comes to the Internet's potential.

It does give all of us access to more information than people of past ages could ever have dreamed of. It does allow us to speak directly with people who we would otherwise have no opportunity to interact with. It does open new doors for learning and collaboration that could not be easily replaced by other means.

But, let's look at what Internet does that isn't so great, and what it *doesn't* do.

The Internet doesn't:

Provide us with face-to-face interaction, which study after study has shown is essential to our mental health.

Though we can rationalize to ourselves that our Internet relationships are every bit as deep and meaningful as face-to-face relationships, the reality is that they simply don't give us cues that our bodies need to be happy - cues such as physical touch, facial expression, and body language.

Face-to-face interactions also *don't* cause the same stress triggers that checking our emails or comment boxes do. Our brain knows how to interpret face-to-face interactions from millennia of evolution - so it doesn't go into them expecting an attack.

Put us in touch with our geographic communities. Although the Internet can help people find people like themselves from all across the world, it *doesn't* do anything to help real-world neighbors connect.

This is important, because many problems - such as physical security, physical infrastructure, etc. - must be addressed by physical communities. Your Internet buddy isn't going to help the little old lady cross the street, bake you a casserole when you're sick, or help support other families in your child's school.

Require that you move around. In fact, the siren song of the computer screen is a powerful impetus *not* to take care of our bodies.

Scientists are beginning to get seriously alarmed by the behavior and physical health of "DigiNatives" who had access to tempting technology in their formative years - many of these young people are not developing basic core muscles and motor skills, and are instead showing a high rate of behaviors associated with anxiety.

It's not that the Internet is a poison - it's that, in many cases, it is completely replacing activities which may be less interesting to us but which are essential to our health as evolved beings.

Prioritize what is important to you. You may be able to use your Internet connection to find work, or educate yourself - but you can also use it to waste immense amounts of time and energy on activities that simply will not be important to you 50 years down the line.

On the other hand, Internet use *does*:

Trigger stress responses in our bodies. Checking your email and arguing online fill you with exactly the same stress hormones you would have in a survival situation.

Used mindfully, and in conjunction with management techniques such as exercise and meditation, it may still be a net gain - but if you're spending hours online each day without stopping periodically to evaluate whether your online activities are really making you *happy* - you may be filled with a lot of unnecessary stress hormones!

My message is not, and will never be, that we should all stop using the Internet. But, as with all of our resources, we must be *conscious* about how we use it if we wish to have the lives we want.

Try:

"Earning" Internet time with behaviors that give you benefits the Internet does not. You can surf the net for an hour, for example - if you exercise, or talk to your neighbor, or cook a healthy meal for an hour first.

Meditating for five minutes at the start of each hour you spend on the computer. You can use this time to calm your breathing (which will become more tense as you spend time engaged with the screen), and prioritize. Ask:

How do the activities I'm doing on this computer make me *feel*? Do I feel deeply fulfilled and happy, or do I feel anxious and impatient?

What tasks on the computer will you benefit in the long run from doing?

Which tasks will you be glad you spent time on 50 years from now, and which will you wish you had spent more time on?

Which tasks will be beneficial to your mental and physical health, and which may be actively detrimental to it?

By making more conscious decisions about our use of technology, we can increase the benefits we get from it - while also *decreasing* the physical effects of technology use, which contribute strongly to our anxiety.

Chapter 4: The Anxious Mind / The Steering Wheel

Now we arrive at the apex of our being: the mind. "Mindfulness" has become a popular buzzword in recent years, and for good reason: making the fullest use of our minds is the easiest way to make sure we are making decisions that will take us where we want to go.

As discussed in previous chapters, the mind is not a standalone entity – how well it functions and how much control we have over it is strongly influenced by the state of our bodies, and our emotional responses which are also strongly influenced by our bodies.

But what do we use to make decisions about how to care for our bodies and our emotions? We use our minds. So the mind is anything but an afterthought – rather, as the Eastern philosophers have always taught, mind and body are one.

Now that we understand how our bodies and emotions can help or hinder our control over our minds, we will talk about how to take charge of our minds directly – of our thoughts about ourselves and the world, and ultimately our decisions about which actions to take.

A Word About Psychotherapy - The perception that it makes you "normal."

I've known many people who had mixed feelings when it comes to psychotherapy. Almost always, when I recommend it to folks, the response is negative. Perhaps this is due to a still-lingering idea that people go to therapy to get "fixed" because they're "crazy."

I find that idea laughably absurd.

Perhaps if one defines "crazy" as "anxious, or depressed, or generally not happy with one's life," it's appropriate to say that therapy is for "crazy" people. But by that definition, do you know anyone who isn't crazy?

Psychotherapy is not part of some identity, the way some people seem to assume. It doesn't mark you as being part of some club, or some class of people who "need therapy." Psychotherapy is a tool - to help you have the life you want to have.

I can't think of many of people I've known who couldn't probably benefit from therapy in some way; I can think of many who I wish would pursue it, because I see how unhappy they are and the challenges they face when they try to tackle these issues alone, without the help of an expert.

Even I, who have often been told that I give pretty good advice, have come to the realization lately that I can't help even my closest friends as much as a therapist would.

I can be there for them, I can support them with all my might, I can be there for them when they need to talk - but interacting with my own therapist has shown me that there's too much I simply don't know about getting to sustainable answers instead of just momentary support.

It is true that there is such a thing as a bad therapist. I have been fortunate enough not to have one, yet - I have only had one who only seemed to tell me what I already knew, and one who turned out to be very, very good.

But I have been advised by multiple friends to "interview" different therapists - and to feel no shame in requesting another, if my first assigned therapist seemed problematic or even just ineffective. This is advice I would pass along to anyone who is considering psychotherapy for the first time.

Perhaps the existence of bad therapists is the reason so many people are reluctant to try psychotherapy - either actively antithetical to it, or feeling that their problems aren't *that* bad to warrant therapy.

Let me tell you - I know quite a few people who I think would be much happier after a year or two of therapy. I've talked to many different types of people about therapy, and seen many different responses to the idea.

There was the teen who wanted nothing to do with it, because a previous experience seeing a therapist with her parents had been bad.

Unfortunately, the family who reacts poorly to therapy or who gives the vibe that they want their child "fixed" is all too common - I may have engaged in therapy earlier if I had not had the sense that the adults in my life wanted me to go to therapy because they wanted feelings that were important to me to change.

There was the young, successful professional woman who approached me quietly one day - we had worked together on a professional project and I had mentioned that I was in therapy.

Upon hearing that, she felt she asked if I thought *she* could perhaps benefit from therapy, as she had been waging a well-hidden battle with anxiety that she worried was developing into depression. My answer was a resounding *yes*.

There was the middle-aged man who had struggled from outbursts of anger all his life. Now, these outbursts were driving his adult children away from him. Could he perhaps get a lifelong habit under control with the assistance of therapy? My answer: you'll never know if you don't try, will you?

Maybe some of you reading this book are already in therapy, and looking for additional techniques to help get you where you want to go. Perhaps some of you feel strongly that therapy is not right for you, for whatever reason. Maybe right now, it's not.

But let this be said: I wish I had started it sooner than I did!

Affirmations – Saying is Believing

Did you know that we can change the shape of our brains - just by thinking?

As with changing the shape of our bodies, this does not happen instantly just because we want it to; it happens little by little, through small exercises that can yield transformative results over time. And isn't a great brain a better reward than a great body?

The reason the brain is able to perform such amazingly diverse tasks as learning and memory is that it is able to form new connections throughout our whole lives. Unlike other organs, which don't change much after we reach adulthood, the brain is always reforming itself.

Learned a new word? That was a new set of synaptic connections being formed. Made a new memory? New connections in the brain.

Buddhist meditation is thought to work so well because it literally rewires the brain - massive size increases in parts of the brain associated with happiness have been found in some Buddhist monks, for example.[12] We will explore meditation - arguably the most powerful tool to learn to consciously manage one's brain and body - in a moment.

But there's also another way to re-wire your brain - and your beliefs about yourself - that also has effects on your mood and performance.

It turns out that simply telling yourself something makes you more likely to believe it. And certain beliefs cause us to perform better - for example, one study found that people who regularly used affirmations to remind themselves of their abilities and competence actually performed better under stress than study participants who did not use affirmations.

Some have suggested that affirmations may have some things in common with ancient practices, such as prayer and magic. Even many religious and occult scholars agree that the important part to a prayer or ritual is bringing your *own* mind in line with reality - not changing the mind of God, or the physical world.

So what sorts of statements make good affirmations? A few simple rules:

Don't use negative statements (such as "is not ___"). This weakens the power of an affirmation. The brain may hear your overall meaning - but it will also hear the negative words. Instead, create positive statements that say what you want them to say without any need for negative language.

Simple statements are easier for the brain to understand. The shorter and simpler your affirmation, the more effective it will be.

Affirmations work best in present tense. For example, saying you "will" do something or that you "have" done something may have an effect - but using your current moment to your advantage is even better!

Affirmations work best if you speak them aloud at least once a day. While "saying" them mentally in a situation where you may not be comfortable saying them aloud, such as an office or classroom, can still help - speaking the words aloud brings them into reality in a way that merely thinking them doesn't.

Many wonderful lists of helpful affirmations exist on the Internet. At the time of this publication, some wonderful sources of affirmations include:

Meditation – Reshape Your Brain and Your Reactions

Meditation has taken on an air of prestige in recent years. It has become "trendy" - which, I suppose, is good. But as with yoga, we have to take great care in our attitudes towards meditation. That which is popular or socially smiled upon tends to become competitive - which is, in fact, debilitating to your meditation practice.

As a child, I had many good experiences with meditation. I was perhaps an odd bird among small children in that I loved to "zone out," as a friend and I called it, to music with a slow, steady beat or slowly evolving melody. My mind would do fascinating things during these times, and I found them immensely relaxing.

Only years later would I learn that several of the techniques we developed paralleled techniques in Buddhist and Hindu meditation. And then, to my great distress, after a few years of foregoing meditation at all due to busy college life - I found I could not seem to get back to those practices.

To start with, even sitting quietly with no distractions felt stressful to adult me.

For reasons I could not pinpoint, even being alone in my quiet dorm room was enough to bring on panic attacks. In hindsight, there were many stressors in my life at that time - I was living alone for the first time, facing tougher classes than I'd ever faced before, and going through a good deal of social turmoil as a result of leaving my old church as well.

Once I got to the point where I was able to sit quietly with no distraction - meditation was not exactly what would happen.

I'd zone out alright - thinking about the day at work, or the last book I'd read, or all of the things on my to-do list. I never seemed to manage to sit for a full five minutes without thinking of something else I really *should* be doing that came to my mind in the quiet and getting up to do it.

This continued for years. Once in a blue moon I'd get in a good meditation session, but those instances seemed to be virtually all due to peer pressure - when my roommate meditated I would meditate with him, and having someone else face-to-face who was meditating with me seemed to help.

Later, I would start going to the local Buddhist temple for the same reason. But I still couldn't seem to meditate at all when I was on my own.

This, it turns out, is quite normal for modern adults. When growing up, in fact, I read literature on meditation and was puzzled by the descriptions in almost every how-to guide counseling me to expect a great deal of chaos and discomfort when I first began. As a child, I never experienced those things. In adulthood, on the other hand - oh boy.

I finally caved in and took a paid meditation class at the local Zen Buddhist Temple after several years of trying to meditate on my own.

I'd long resisted the idea of paying someone to teach me how to do something that I had done successfully before - but my attempts to meditate on my own time were not working, with meditation ending up feeling like just one more chore. I couldn't seem to get relaxed, and the harder I tried, the less relaxing my meditation was.

In the class, I began to get an inkling of what I was doing wrong. As you may have guessed from reading earlier chapters - I was neglecting the vital communication between my mind and my body. I was insistent on trying to force my mind into a state of calm, insisting that meditation was only a *mental* exercise - when this was decidedly not the case.

In our meditation classes, here's what our teacher did that really changed things:

Belly breathing. There was no rushing through the breathing portion of meditation for my teacher. Which, frankly, was probably why I always failed on my own.

"Rushing" and "meditation" are as antithetical to each other as water and fire - the whole point of meditation is to remove the brain from the "just survive" mindset that the onslaught of daily tasks tends to put us into. So "hurry up and meditate" makes even less sense than "hurry up and sleep."

So for the first five minutes of our class, the teacher was very strict about this: we were to lie on our backs on yoga mats (a regular floor will work too, though mattresses not so well) and practice belly breathing.

Breathing into the belly has been called "the most relaxing thing you can do." It relaxes many muscles and sends calming signals to the brain. To achieve this, our teacher instructed that we keep our chests flat and breath by inflating and deflating our lower bellies. But what really helped for me was envisioning my "center."

In Eastern thought, there's a point in the "center" of our bodies from which all of our energy flows. It's located in the lower belly, perhaps an inch below the belly button and two inches behind it.

While that point initially sounded arbitrary when I was told about it, practicing convinced me that there was something to this discovery.

Envisioning my breath flowing to and from this area gave me a depth of sensation I was not able to achieve otherwise, and I found that my mental image of the breath flowing into my center would fluctuate, sometimes flowing in different patterns from the ones I'd intended - as though it really were measuring some sort of mental or physical process.

This five minutes per day of belly breathing was probably the most important thing to my mindfulness and meditation practice. Envisioning the flow of breath to and from my center was crucial to this - focusing on the mechanics of breathing alone simply didn't work.

So regardless of whether you are trying to establish a meditation practice, or just trying to bring yourself down from the week - try five minutes of belly breathing each day to reap the benefits!

Body scan. After our five minutes of belly breathing, our teacher would guide us through a "body scan." Starting with our toes, we would take turns bringing awareness to each part of our body in turn.

This brought our conscious awareness to areas of tension in our bodies - and often, simply focusing on them would do a great deal to alleviate them. This process probably took about another five minutes.

Stretching. I had enjoyed stretching, particularly yoga-style stretching, from an early age. Following a back injury in my early adulthood,

I had almost entirely stopped doing it.

Our yoga teacher would have us begin with some mild yoga stretches before assuming our seated meditation positions. This facilitated us sitting up straight - the best posture to promote conscious awareness - without excessive stress or discomfort.

Some of the most useful exercises, which I will not attempt to explain here, were hip openers and a sun salutation. Try YouTubing these two types of exercises for how-to demonstrations!

Sitting postures. Zen Buddhist monks have had literally millennia to perfect the art of sitting up straight for long periods of time without too much thinking or discomfort. Among the things I learned from them were:

Have a meditation cushion. These cushions are firmer and thicker than regular pillows - cushions made especially for meditation are ideal, but I've made due with two or three regular couch or bed cushions stacked atop each other.

Sitting with your butt on the cushion and your feet off the floor will take pressure of the lower spine and ease circulation to the legs, making it easy to sit in a restful, erect posture where you don't have to think too much about staying upright.

Stable postures. Turns out it's not just that chairs weren't fashionable in ancient Asia - sitting in a chair requires some degree of concentration to keep one's balance.

Meditation postures, such as the full-, half-, and quarter-lotus postures, are designed to provide a stable foundation by distributing one's weight across three points of contact with the ground or cushion: your butt or the base of your spine, and each knee.

It turns out I'm a quarter-lotus person myself - that posture being much like sitting "cross legged" or "Indian style" as you probably learned in school. Other practitioners preferred to kneel with the cushion upright in between their legs, supporting their upper bodies.

Try YouTubing "meditation postures" for more visual guides to how to sit in stable, erect relaxation.

Chapter 5 – Draw Your Own Road Map, Choose Your Destination

The self-actualized individual, it is said, is the person whose existence is not defined by the circumstances they are thrown into. It is the person who, rather than just reacting, *decides* who they want to be and where they want to go. And then does it.

The psychologist Maslow taught that self-actualization stood at the top of a "hierarchy of needs" – physical needs, emotional needs, and psychological needs that needed to be fulfilled before a person could have the necessary tools to become the conscious shaper of their own life and identity.

Modern science has shown us that, to some extent, Maslow was right – that the physical needs of our brains, the emotional needs of our hearts, and the psychological needs of our hearts can all make it harder or easier for us to see all the possibilities within our grasp, and to take action to seize those possibilities.

Now, in this book, we have discussed how to meet the needs of our bodies. We have discussed how to create a healthy emotional life. We have discussed how to re-shape our brains, to have more conscious control over where we go.

Now it's time to talk about how to choose what destination we really want to pursue – and how to make choices every day that keep us moving along the roads we want to travel.

Where Do You Want to Be?

Very often, we take a reactive view of life. "X happened - how can I cope with it?" How can I cope with my husband snapping at me? How can I cope with my stressful job? How can I cope with my chronic illness?

These questions certainly do need to be answered - life will *always* contain both joy and pain, will always give us things to cope with.

Many people ask us, in making our decisions, to focus on what we *want*. This is useful, as there are some desires that differ between people.

I, for example, love the idea of writing novels - others I've spoken to think that sounds like something they could never do. I don't enjoy doing math - but other people I have known find it to be their true passion. Some people like nothing more than the idea of settling down and having children - others don't want to have children at all.

But other desires may be more universal. Who doesn't want a great relationship? A job that affords both freedom and a hefty retirement fund? A reputation for great skill in an area we're passionate about?

This is why it's very important to learn - sometimes through trial and error - what is important to us. Some people really do prefer the perks of a stable desk job that allows for a stable family life and community participation. Others are more passionate about a mission in life, be it art, science, or charity.

In this next chapter, we'll discuss the precious resources that are our time, energy, money, and willpower - and how to sustainably budget our precious existence to prioritize that which deeply fulfills us.

You are Your Most Important Resource - How to Budget with Spoons

If you frequent social media, you may be familiar with "Spoon Theory" - the idea that people have a finite amount of energy to work with each day. The use of "how many spoons you have" as a metaphor for energy levels was originated by the writer Christine Miserandino, who writes about "invisible" illnesses - those without immediately obvious physical symptoms.

Miserandino's writing began with lupus - an autoimmune disease in which the body attacks its own organs, often without "classical" symptoms of illness such as coughing, sneezing, etc.. But her Spoon Theory has since been used by people with all manner of chronic illnesses such as autism, depression, and anxiety.

In spoon theory, it is assumed that perfectly healthy people have a never-ending supply of spoons that they can use to get dressed, brush their hair, brush their teeth, socialize, perform tasks at work, etc..[15]

The idea of having limited spoons seems to resonate with an increasing number of people in our modern era where people are often faced with countless expectations and have to choose which ones to satisfy, even in a state of perfect health - and an increasing number of people suffer from depression and anxiety.

I know from firsthand experience as a result of having friends with chronic illnesses that for most people, their anxiety levels do not rival the toll on one's "spoons" posed by conditions such as lupus, stroke, or autism. But I still find the concept of "spoons" very useful for working with questions of energy and willpower.

Science has shown that willpower is, indeed, a finite quantity. The way they tested this was rather hilarious – research volunteers were made to wait in a room scented with the smell of fresh-baked chocolate chip cookies. They were then brought into a room where plates of both delicious baked goods and radishes were laid out. Some volunteers were asked to eat the radishes, while others got to indulge in the cookies.

Those who had to eat radishes while watching other volunteers eat cookies did worse on subsequent willpower tests than those who had been allowed to eat the cookies! This proved empirically that there was a relationship between the amount of willpower used on one task – resisting cookies, in this case – and the amount of willpower that was available for other tasks.[14]

But the results are important: people do, indeed, have finite spoons - and those some people have more spoons than others, no one has an infinite supply.

So the road to good mental health, weather you have a serious chronic illness that depletes your "spoons" or merely the challenges of everyday life, is budgeting with spoons. This means a few things.

The recognition that we have a finite supply of energy and willpower tells us something else that's very important. It tells us that we must consciously choose our priorities, if we wish to be able to consciously choose the shape of our lives.

For some this may seem simple enough: prioritizing school performance, or a job that they love, for example. But for many of us, the picture becomes much more complicated. Do we spend time on a hobby that relaxes us right now, or on a long-term effort to get into a job we like better than the one we have right now? Surely a little bit of each is required - how much of each?

How do we decide which jobs to pursue - is it the one that pays the most, as conventional wisdom states, or are there other factors about our work that are more important to us? How do we decide how to budget our social spoons? Do we have friends who always seem to leave us feeling down or exhausted? Do we have friends who don't?

This is where spoon budgeting becomes an art.

I face some of these problems on a daily basis. Because the Internet provides instant gratification, my brain often wants to spend time - which is a form of spoons - on online hobbies such as chatrooms. But, do these chatrooms do me any good at all in the long run?

Once in a blue moon, a conversation with good ideas comes out of one. But chatrooms ultimately need to be prioritized behind both of my jobs, my meditation classes, exercise, visiting friends, and other basic self-care tasks such as cooking and doing dishes. And all of those things have to be prioritized relative to each other as well.

Some days, I just don't have enough spoons to exercise or socialize or do the dishes. On those day, my spoons go first to my two jobs, then to my meditation - then exercise if I have spoons left, etc..

This is my personal order of allocating spoons, to ensure that I do the tasks that are most important to my personal long-term satisfaction first.

What's your preferred order of allocating spoons?

Try this:

Ask, where do you want to be five years from now? Ten years? Twenty? Fifty?

Choose the time frame that seems best to you. If you're a high school or college student, you may not have any idea where you want to be in twenty years - and rightly so!

If you're a young professional tackling the Big Questions of career, family, and relationships, fifty years may be the time frame you really want to pay attention to.

For whatever your chosen time frame is, write five things you want to have in your life at that time. Do good grades make the list? A hefty retirement fund? A loving spouse? Children or grandchildren? Mad skillz or prestige in an art you're passionate about?

If you're having trouble narrowing it down – perhaps you really do want it *all*, art, science, family, career – consider the wonderful work of Mark Manson, who has reframed the question of "What Do You Want?" in a way that's a little more down-to-Earth here:

http://www.markmanson.net/question

Once you have your five, ten, or fifty year desire - consider what should be your top five priorities *now* to get there. **Rank them in order.**

As with all budgeting in life, spending spoons on one task will leave you with fewer spoons for another. So give some serious thought to which outcomes are most important to you.

It may be that you can have both a hefty retirement fund and a career in the field which you love; but in case you can't, which would you rather have at the expense of the other? Your top priority gets priority for spoons in the here and now.

Consciously choosing your goals and making a list that you can use to allocate your spoons every day helps ensure that you are not just reacting to chaotic events - you are actively shaping your life and choosing its contents.

There may be sacrifices to make. I had to cut way back on my social engagements - in groups where some people already felt I didn't spend enough time with them - to do the work necessary for a career transition and a renewed meditation practice.

But was my life better after I made those priority decisions? Absolutely.

No, Really. Take Care of Your Spoons.

The biggest risks for people working to shape their futures in the face of mental health challenges come in two flavors. As with honoring vs. managing your emotions, it's a delicate dance: you may expect too much of yourself and burn out, or you may not expect enough and subsequently not take the actions necessary to realize your potential.

That makes it difficult to give advice to people struggling with anxiety that will be universal. Some people will inevitably say "but you can't expect me to get up off the couch, my life is too hard for that!" others will say "but I didn't completely transform my life in the first week, clearly I am a failure and there's no point to trying!"

Both of these attitudes are counter to the real world. In the real world, we have the power to change our lives - and indeed, if we don't, no one else will. But in the real world, change never comes instantly, or easily - and things never go exactly as planned.

Before entering therapy, I fell more into the "my life is too hard for that!" category. Constantly tired (due to an untreated medical condition, it turned out) and stressed (due to some issues that were worked through with my therapist), I didn't understand how anyone could expect me to change my life.

How could I ever get the career I wanted when I was already scrambling for time and money, even with many things working in my favor? How could I be expected to go through all the paperwork, all the learning, the *extra* investment of time and energy to start building a portfolio while still working full-time in another field?

But after therapy and medication, I became the second type of person - the type who *knows* their fate rests in their own hands, and as a result, blames themselves for every little thing that does not go according to plan.

I was having trouble working on my writing because I was upset about something someone said? Why did I have to be so easily upset?! I was having trouble exercising because I was super-tired? Why couldn't I have more energy?!

It took quite a few instances of my older, wiser neighbor pointing out to me to realize that I was making no room for my (healthy) emotions ("Yes, you should be upset by someone saying something so offensive!", my body's physical needs ("If you don't have energy today, you don't have energy - and you just have to accept that."

I still walk the line, to be sure, between expecting too little of myself, and not expecting enough. I've been walking the line for long enough now, and with enough help from wise and educated people, that I know *I* am the boss of my own expectations for myself. Whether I am doing "enough" to improve my life - is defined strictly by me.

Am I happy with the outcomes? Then I am succeeding?

Am I unhappy with the outcomes? What can I change about what I'm doing? What can I *actually* change, in a world where superhumanly augmenting my brain and becoming a cyborg is not an option?

The bottom line is, your spoons are precious. Your spoons are only yours, and there is a finite supply of them. If you don't have more spoons, being frustrated with yourself for running out of energy is about as productive as being frustrated with yourself for not being able to conjure dollar bills out of thin air.

But if you find that you consistently don't have the spoons necessary to achieve your desired standard of well-being - you may wish to seriously examine how you are spending your spoons.

Are you spending a lot of time on activities that are emotionally and cognitively taxing, but which bring you no long-term benefit? Are you letting others peer pressure you into spending spoons in a way that you know is not productive for your long-term goals? Are there actions you could take to help you manage your spoons, such as seeking therapy, that you haven't taken yet?

On the other side of the line, are you being too hard on yourself? Are you neglecting self-care and personal time to the point that you are at risk of burning out?

Only you know the answer to these questions. But really, take care of your spoons.

Here are a few simple ways to respect your spoons - and your own authority to make decisions about them:

Having a low-spoon day? Go out of your way to spend your time relaxing. You are allowed to relax. You deserve it.

Having a high-spoon day? Make it an investment. Devote some

spoons to exercise, if at all possible - as exercise will raise your overall spoon level.

Having a low-spoon couple of weeks? Take an inventory of where your spoons are going. Try making a list of how you have spent time and energy each day of your low-spoon period. What could you do to save spoons? Are you using the few you do have in a the way that's most productive for your long-term well-being?

Remember - No one but you gets to decide how you spend your spoons. Not those friends who want you to go out drinking, not those family members who think you should spend more time on your hair and makeup.

You have more power - to help yourself, and ultimately help others by developing your own unique potential - by being in control of your spoons than you possibly could be by pleasing someone else in the short term!

Because this is a lot to think about, here are some spoon-specific affirmations to help you cherish your spoons in an easy way:

My life is my own. I make conscious choices to shape my destiny.

I love and approve of myself.

Today, I am brimming with energy and potential!

I know myself. No one else knows what is best for me.

I am human. Imperfection is part of the glory of being human.

I make choices to shape the life I want to have.

I feel the love of many who cherish me, seen and unseen.

I treat my time and energy with reverence.

Now that you've had an overview of this library of tools for managing anxiety – on the last two pages, we have provided a sample menu of activities, and a template for a weekly worksheet that you may find helpful to assist you in gradually incorporating helpful habits in your life over time.

Remember – your relationship with your mind, body, and emotions takes ongoing work, listening, and communication - just like any other relationship.

With the proper management tools, your mind, body, and emotions can make a stellar team to take you where you want to go. But like any relationship, it's not all business – your mind, body, and emotions should enjoy each other!

Example Activity Menu

- Belly breathing – 5 mins

- Exercise of your choice - 20 mins

- Hydrate with water

- Cook healthy

- Healthy snack break

- Schedule 8 hours for sleep

- Body scan – how is my body feeling? How can I address it?

- Mindful emotions – How is my relationship with my emotions today? Am I ignoring them? Are they ruling me?

- Aromatherapy break

- Music break

- Sitting meditation – 10 mins

- Affirmation break

- Mindful technology – Stop every 20, 30, or 60 minutes and evaluate your state of mind. Is your use of technology making your life better? Is it benefiting your 1-, 5-, or 50- year plan?

- Mindful technology – Practice 5 minutes of walking or sitting meditation for every hour you spend on the computer. This will manage your stress signals and keep the neurotransmitters flowing.

- Journal – Where do you want to be to be a year from now? Five years? Fifty? How can you work towards that goal tomorrow?

- Journal – Budget your spoons. What are your top three priorities to reach your 1-, 5-, or 50-year goal? How will you prioritize your time and energy tomorrow to ensure that these happen?

- Self-care – Make half an hour for yourself. Just for yourself.

Weekly Worksheet

Example	<ul><li>9am - Start the day with 5 mins orange oil aromatherapy</li><li>12pm - 5 mins orange oil aromatherapy!</li><li>3pm - 5 mins orange oil aromatherapy!</li><li>6pm - 5 mins orange oil aromatherapy!</li></ul>
Sun	
Mon	
Tues	
Wed	
Thurs	
Fri	
Sat	

www.ingramcontent.com/pod-product-compliance
Lightning Source LLC
Chambersburg PA
CBHW021350160726
47994CB00007B/2901